DERBY
City Beautiful

DERBY
City Beautiful

Alistair and Jan Campbell

breedon **books**

PUBLISHING

First published in Great Britain in 2008 by
The Breedon Books Publishing Company Limited
Breedon House, 3 The Parker Centre,
Derby, DE21 4SZ.

A catalogue record for this book is available from
the British Library.

ISBN 978-1-85983-622-4

Printed and bound by Progress Press, Malta.

CONTENTS

DEDICATION

This book is dedicated to all
our family and friends, especially
Lisa, Lindsay and *Ruby.*

FOREWORD

There is something really special about Derby. Located right in the centre of England on the banks of the River Derwent and set within stunning countryside, it is a pleasant, compact city that has punched well above its weight for centuries, especially in the field of arts, science and wealth-creation. For over 2,000 years many have been attracted to Derby, from world conquerors – the Romans no less – to today's world icon Rolls-Royce.

Derby is unique. It's the only city name you will find listed in a dictionary – an adjective forever associated with intense local rivalry, be it in Milan or Manchester, plus, of course, the world famous horse race. One of our most talented sons, Joseph Wright of Derby, adopted his hometown nomenclature along with only one other artist, Leonardo Da Vinci.

Derby's history is littered with famous names and events, from Bonnie Prince Charlie and his fateful 'decision in Derby' in 1745, through to being the birthplace of the Industrial Revolution, as well as that most contemporary of phenomena Lara Croft. Recognised by UNESCO as being home to the world's first factory, Derby also gave England its first public park – a city of innovative ideas and practice shaped by the likes of Gibbs, Bass, Darwin and Pugin.

The beautiful pictures contained in this book are nothing short of a revelation. They help the reader to appreciate the city in a new way. Many reinforce how important it is to look up, above the street level, and really see the city as never before. The commentary reveals another layer of our exotic heritage: our 'palais de danse', 'cour d'honneur' and 'baldachinno'; Italian assassinations or Derby's contribution to winning the Battle of Britain.

Today Derby is attracting massive investment in order to bring much of its infrastructure into the 21st century. The city still sells its wares across the globe and today's Derbeians come from all corners of the world. This book celebrates Derby as it is today, a city proud of our past and confident for our future.

JOHN FORKIN
DIRECTOR
MARKETING DERBY

Glasgow   London   Cardiff

www. UKCity Images .com

Alistair and Jan Campbell are the founders and principal photographers of UK City Images. This elite and independent image library specialises in providing the travel and media industries with high-quality photographs of UK city scenes and landmarks.

Portraying the richness and diversity of UK city architecture helps promote Britain as a desirable tourist destination, to both a global and British audience. Images are captured in a style that is deliberately designed to excite positive interest in their location and history.

All images within this publication are the sole copyright of UK City Images, who are pleased to offer a facility to purchase either print or data copies to both commercial and private customers. Sales enquiries should be directed to sales@ukcityimages.com.

An exciting array of other UK city scenes and landmarks, plus additional Derby images, can be viewed from our website at **www.ukcityimages.com**.

Liverpool   Birmingham   Newcastle   Portsmouth

INTRODUCTION

INDUSTRIA, VIRTUS, ET FORTITUDO
DILIGENCE, COURAGE, STRENGTH

Located within the county of Derbyshire and in close proximity to the Peak District National Park, Derby owes much of its status as a city to its long and enthralling history.

Its journey from settlement to city began over 2,000 years ago. The city's unique position at the lowest crossing point on the River Derwent was recognised as a strategic military location by an invading Roman army. The tactical importance of the site was later verified, first by Saxon occupation, then by Viking conquest. The name of Derby is believed to be either a translation from the Danish Deoraby – the village of the deer – or, alternatively, to be derived from the name for the original Roman settlement, Derventio. Regardless of its early foundations, the city's influence on both British and global history is both disproportional and, perhaps, unappreciated by many who have little or no knowledge of Derby's unique heritage.

A stroll around the mediaeval streets and riverside will give a fascinating insight into the city's involvement in civil war, public riots and an aborted expedition to overthrow the King of England. Further exploration will unveil tales of industrial revolution and espionage, a UNESCO World Heritage site and the hefty human price Derbeians paid for their engineering ingenuity during World War Two.

Ancient religious structures, exceptional architectural craftsmanship and contrasting building materials and styles are prevalent throughout the city's streets and lanes, where you will also discover statues and public art honouring princes, nurses, brewers and artists. A recent £2 billion-pound investment programme has transformed the inner-city landscape. The city now proudly boasts the largest modern retail complex in the East Midlands, which is further complimented with an abundance of traditional daily produce, local farmers' and continental markets.

Finding solitude from the bustling streets, lanes and shops is easily achieved in any one of Derby's 300 open public spaces and parks, one of which claims to be England's first public park and was reputedly used as a model for New York's Central Park. Globally renowned for its industrial heritage, Derby continues to prosper as a thriving hi-technology-based major employer in the aerospace, railway engineering, car production, clockmaking and high-quality porcelain industries.

Each page of *Derby City Beautiful* colourfully and aesthetically portrays a scene, personality, landmark or tradition associated with this unique and historic city. Collectively the images offer a creative perspective and stunning portfolio, which certifies that Derby is truly a 'City Beautiful'.

DERBY'S CENTRAL STREETS

A significant proportion of Derby's city centre is considered to be of special architectural or historical interest, with much of the central district being designated a Conservation Area. This protective status requires that local planning authorities consider the character and appearance of these areas when structural or environmental changes are proposed. However, prior to this building legislation, some of the city centre streets were partially demolished to cope with increased traffic flow. Despite a street-widening programme in the late 19th century and a late 20th-century inner ring road project, the city has retained numerous areas and structures of particular historical merit, with its central streets maintaining mediaeval links, both in name and appearance. Although Derby is a city of contrasting architectural styles and construction materials, there does seem to be a prevalent theme of curves amoung its streets and lanes. The scope of this publication does not allow the space to feature all of Derby's unique history and heritage. However, although not intended to be a definitive guide, the following chapters illustrate a few of the many streets, lanes, structures and buildings that are particularly worthy of note within the city centre. Further personal exploration will reveal even more.

Cathedral Quarter

Derby has designated the city centre into specific cultural districts. It is particularly proud of the Cathedral Quarter, which includes much of the city's mediaeval heritage. The name 'gate' is attached to many of the Cathedral Quarter's central streets and is the Danish translation of 'street'. A rich café and friendly social scene prevails throughout the whole area, ensuring that visitors have the opportunity to mix cultural and retail encounters with refreshment and nourishment. The following images illustrate many of the areas included within the Cathedral Quarter.

Commissioned by Derby City Council to create a water sculpture for the refurbished Market Place, the artist William Pye designed a York stone feature that enabled visitors to walk behind the cascading water and experience the sensation of looking through an actual waterfall. Part of Derby's Public Artwork Trail, the waterfall is more formally known as the 'Market Place Water Feature'. Since its completion in 1995 the water feature has proved to be very popular with children.

View of the Guildhall in the Market Place from the top of the waterfall.

Market Place

With its history of market trading, entertainment, criminal punishment and conducting local government business, the Market Place is Derby's principle civic square and inner-city public space. Many of the city's central streets run towards or away from the square, making it an ideal starting point to begin exploring the city centre and riverside.

Standing on top of the Market Place waterfall looking across the square will offer an elevated vision of the architectural diversity that is prevalent throughout the city.

In addition to the World War One memorial and the Derby Promenade Waterfall, the square is also home to early and modern architecture, with its oldest building dating from approximately 300 years ago and its newest incumbent, the Quad, being completed in 2008. The square is also home to the Tourist Information Centre, which is situated on the corner of the Assembly Rooms.

Derby's prominence as a market town dates from the 12th century, with the Market Place being the site of regular markets until 1933 when it was relocated, first to the Morledge then eventually to its new home in the Eagle Centre. However, the tradition of holding markets in the Market Square still prevails, with periodical open-air farmers' and continental markets.

Evening view of the Promenade Fountain.

Assembly Rooms

Completed in 1977, the Assembly Rooms replaced the 17th-century Newcastle House and Assembly Rooms, which were destroyed by fire in 1963. The façade of the gutted building was rescued and reconstructed in the National Tramway Village at Crich. Constructed to a design by Casson and Condor, the Assembly Rooms are considered Derby's premier indoor live entertainment complex. The venue is home to a packed programme of art and entertainment. Its main arena, the Great Hall, has a maximum capacity of approximately 2,000.

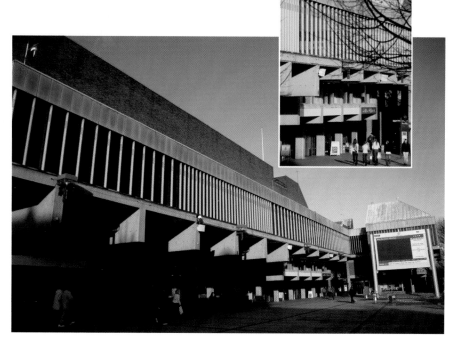

Assembly Rooms Great Hall.

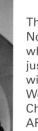

Market Place War Memorial

The memorial was erected in the Market Place on 11 November 1924 to commemorate the men of Derby who died in World War One. A bronze sword of justice was later added to the rear of the memorial, with additional plaques honouring those who fell in World War Two and later conflicts. Designed by Charles Thompson and sculpted by Arthur Walker ARA, the bronze figures are mounted on a stone plinth outside the Guildhall.

Guildhall

The Guildhall, now the Guildhall Theatre, is arguably one of Derby's most distinctive landmarks. Dating from 1483, the present Guildhall has had four predecessors, with its immediate ancestor being destroyed by fire in 1841. Rebuilt the following year, the structure was continually utilised for town council business for over 100 years. A period of structural dilapidation followed the council's 1949 move to larger purpose-built premises on Corporation Street. Plans to convert the building to the Guildhall Theatre were finally realised in 1971. Proud of its diverse programme of amateur and professional productions, this enchanting bijou theatre has a total capacity just short of 250. The theatre's impressive façade is complimented internally with an attractive entrance staircase and an ornate plaster ceiling in the auditorium.

Market Place War Memorial.

THE GREAT WAR
1914 – 1918

Guildhall with the Market Place waterfall in the foreground.

Silhouetted view of the weather vane on top of the Guildhall roof.

The theatre auditorium.

Overleaf: An attractive ornate plaster ceiling is suspended high above the theatre auditorium.

The Guildhall
Theatre staircase,
which leads from
the entrance hall to
the auditorium.

Derby's new Visual Arts and
Media Centre, the Quad.

View north from the Market Place
waterfall towards Iron Gate.

Iron Gate

Looking north from the Market Place along Iron Gate, the view is dominated by the Cathedral Church of All Saints. This street was the birthplace of the Derby artist Joseph Wright and was also the principal manufacturing district for blacksmiths. Described in the 1700s as a street of 'inns and shopkeepers', the area has maintained its traditional commercial inheritance. With 19th-century structural alteration on the west side and much of the east side of the street demolished to widen the road, Iron Gate has managed to retain much of its character and charm.

Evening view of Iron Gate with Derby Cathedral in the background.

The rebuilt east side of Iron Gate.

Iron Gate's Standing Order pub, which was formerly a bank.

Evening view of the Derby All Saints Cathedral at the northern end of Iron Gate.

Joseph Wright Memorial

The Joseph Wright memorial obelisk was erected in 1992 to commemorate the birthplace of the Derby artist. The orrery topping the obelisk depicts the scientific instrument featured in one of Wright's most notable works *A Philosopher Lecturing on the Orrery*.

Joseph Wright memorial obelisk.

Queen Street

Heading north from the top of Iron Gate is Queen Street, which begins its vista with Derby's oldest public house and ends with a distant view of the Gothic-style St Mary's Church.

The Dolphin Inn

At the junction of Full Street, Iron Gate and Queen Street is Derby's oldest public house. Ye Olde Dolphin Inn has apparently been licensed to sell its wares since 1530. There are also local rumours relating to the inn being haunted by several ghosts.

Full Street

East from the corner of Queen Street and Full Street is another Derby hostelry, known as the Silk Mill Inn. Painted on its side wall is a large mural depicting the 1833–34 trade union dispute, during which workers were discriminated against for belonging to a trade union. The mural was created in 1986 by the Derby Community Arts Project.

Ye Old Dolphin Inn with Derby Cathedral in the background.

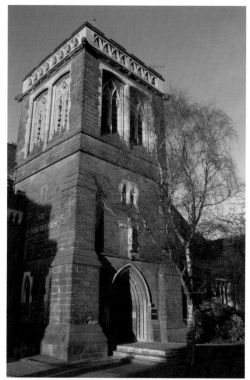

Believed to be built on the site of a church dating from the time of the Norman Conquest, St Michael's Church, built in 1858, has been converted to commercial office space.

Distant view of Augustus Pugin's St Mary's Church, with the St Alkmund footbridge in the foreground.

Sadler Gate

Leading from the Market Place and Iron Gate to the Strand, the mediaeval Sadler Gate is believed to originate from an early 13th-century Danish settlement. As its name suggests, it is supposedly named after the predominant craft originally produced in the street. Along its exceptionally contrasting architectural expanse there are excellent examples of 18th and 19th-century structures, with lanes leading off to a Victorian arcade and ancient yards. This long, curving street contains many individual specialised retail outlets. The pedestrianised route is also home to a selection of pubs, clubs, alfresco cafés, bistros and restaurants, all of which ensure the area's popularity as a vibrant daytime and evening social venue.

An 18th-century red-brick building converted to a bank on the corner of Iron Gate and Sadler Gate.

Contrasting architecture and retail shop signs along the south side of Sadler Gate.

Evening view of Sadler Gate looking west.

A restoration project in 1929 added the timbering to this early 18th-century former coaching inn, now the Old Bell Hotel.

View of shops and cafés looking east up Sadler Gate.

Old Blacksmiths Yard

Known previously as Palfree's Yard, Old Blacksmiths Yard has been converted to an attractive square with offices, restaurants and bars.

Evening view of Old Blacksmiths Yard.

Magistrates' Court.

St Mary's Gate

With the principal church at one end and law and order represented at the other, St Mary's Gate is steeped in history and has been, in the past, the scene of civil unrest and riots. Traditionally referred to as the legal quarter, the street originally contained a mixture of residential properties, a hotel, magistrate's court and quarters, plus also financial and legal services. The recent opening of a new boutique-style hotel and the conversion of the former Shire Hall to a Magistrate's Court partially reverts the street to its former glory and purpose. Perhaps the most formidable building is the 1660 County Hall or Shire Hall, now the Magistrates' Court, which is fronted by a large courtyard formerly known as a cour d'honneur, where royal proclamations and election results would be read out. This building's long history offers an enthralling account of the British Assize legal system, which was abolished in 1971 and replaced by the Crown Courts.

St Mary's Gate Hotel.

Opposite: Derby All Saints' Cathedral at the top of St Mary's Gate.

The Wardwick

Reputedly the oldest recorded street name in Derby, the Wardwick progressively transformed from Walda's Dairy Farm to a predominately residential area. Now a combination of residential, office and retail properties, the street contains some fine 17th, 18th and 19th-century architecture and is home to Derby's first brick building, the Jacobean House. Museum Square, the city library and the former Mechanics' Institute are also situated on this short thoroughfare.

The former Mechanics Institute.

Opposite: The 1879 Gothic-style main entrance to the Central Library.

Jacobean House.

Museum Square

Sculpted by the renowned Sir J.E. Boehm, a statue of the brewer and philanthropist Sir Michael Thomas Bass is the prominent feature within Museum Square. The statue of the former MP for Derby was originally erected in the Market Place but, due to a street widening project, was later moved in 1925 to its present Museum Square location.

The Strand

The culverting of Markeaton and Bramble brooks enabled the creation of a new Derby street, The Strand. Completed in 1881, this gently meandering street with decorated masonry was designed by Giles & Brookhouse as a commercial venture for the wealthy railway contractor Sir Abraham Woodiwiss, who was also the Mayor of Derby 1880–82. Linking the Strand to Sadler Gate, the Strand Arcade was designed by J.S. Story and is said to be based on London's Burlington Arcade. Woodiwiss also donated land on the southern side of the Strand, which enabled, with the financial help of Thomas Bass, an extension to be built to the Museum and Art Gallery.

View of Number 1 The Strand from Victoria Street.

Architectural detail of Number 1 The Strand.

The Strand.

Number 1
The Strand.

The Strand.

Strand Arcade façade.

Corn Market

The pedestrianised Corn Market stretches from Market Square to the corner of Victoria Street and Albert Street. Like many of Derby's central streets, the Corn Market was widened to cope with increased traffic in 1877. In addition to the sale of grains, the area was previously utilised for many commercial and civic purposes, including the editing of the *Derby Evening Telegraph*, and was the location of a 16th-century gaol which was demolished in 1757.

The street contains many fine buildings, including the Joseph Pickford-designed former Tiger Inn. The corner of Victoria Street and Albert Street offers a fine example of the architectural curves that feature throughout the city. This position also allows views beyond Corn Market of the former Debenhams building, the Athenaeum Rooms (Royal Buildings) and, in the opposite direction, the Corn Exchange, all of which are worthy of further visual scrutiny.

Royal Building

Stretching along Victoria Street from the corner of Corn Market and the Strand are the Royal Buildings, which were built in 1837–39 to the designs of Robert Wallace. The Grade II-listed group of buildings includes the former Royal Hotel, the Athenaeum Rooms and the Post Office, which are located in Victoria Street.

Left: The old Royal Hotel.

Below left: The former Royal Hotel and Athenaeum Rooms on Victoria Street.

Below: The Athenaeum Rooms on Victoria Street.

The Royal Building ex-Post Office.

Bearing a plaque dating 1848, the building on the corner of Corn Market and Albert Street is now a retail jewellers. This was in the past, the site of Robert and Alice Liversage's house. Robert was a wealthy businessman in the wool dyeing trade. He donated much of his wealth to the local community especially his local parish St Peters. He is also credited with providing funds to build the cathedral tower.

The former site of
Robert Liversage's
home.

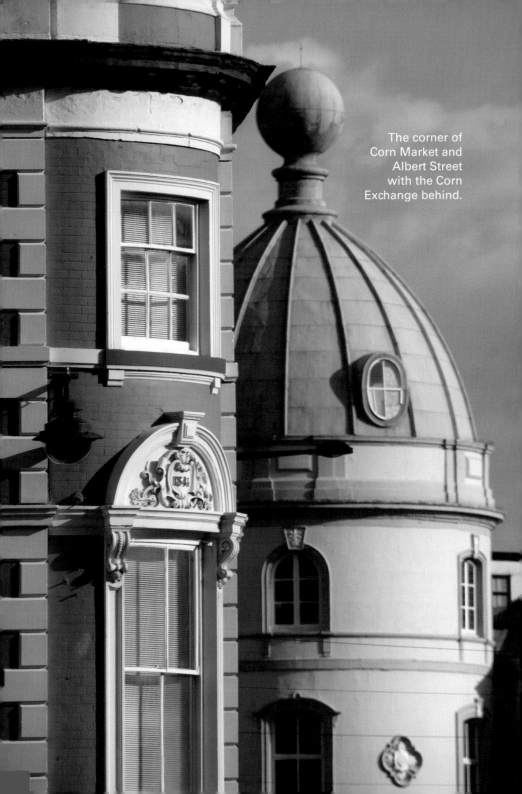

The corner of Corn Market and Albert Street with the Corn Exchange behind.

Corn Exchange

Prior to the construction of the Corn
Exchange in 1862, the buying and selling of corn had previously been conducted
in Corn Market. Situated on the junction of Exchange Street and Albert Street, the
exchange offered a versatile business and entertainment complex. Since the
Corn Exchange Company ceased trading in 1881 the building has had a variety
of uses, including theatre of varieties, dance hall (Palais de Danse), *Derby
Evening Telegraph* offices, private offices and commercial snooker room.

The Lanes

A mixture of retail, leisure and professional services occupy 'the Lanes', which have become known locally as 'Derby's hidden gems'. The Lanes consist of Green Lane, Babington Lane, St Peter's Churchyard and Gower Street.

View of Green Lane from Victoria Street.

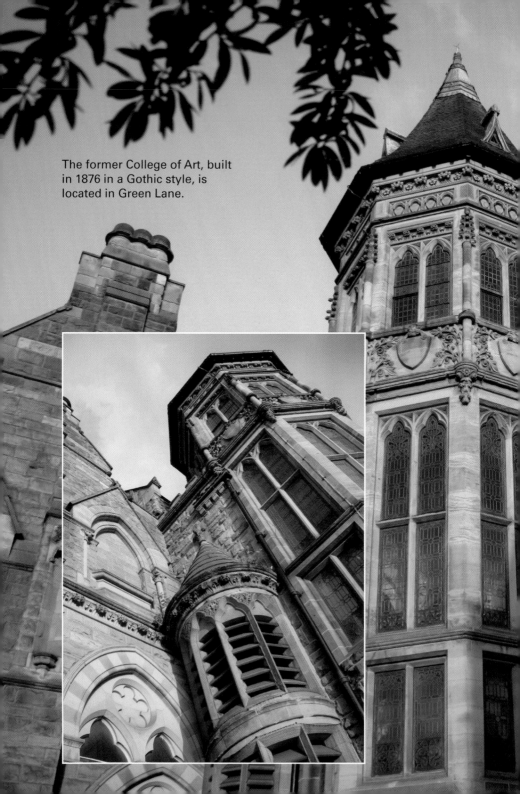

The former College of Art, built in 1876 in a Gothic style, is located in Green Lane.

St Peter's Street

Supposedly named after its principal church, St Peter's Street leads directly across from the Corn Market up a gently sloping hill towards the Spot. Home to the 11th-century St Peter's Church and Churchyard, the street and its connecting thoroughfares contain many fine buildings with intricate and interesting façades. Most of this primarily retail district is pedestrianised.

View looking down
St Peter's Street.

Dating from approximately 1042, parts of St Peter's Church are thought to be almost 1,000 years old, making it the oldest church in Derby. Traces of its Saxon ancestry are still evident within the church.

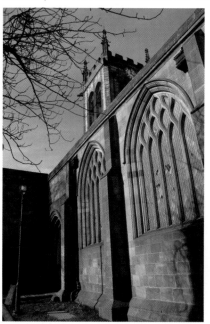

A short sequence of late Victorian buildings in St Peter's Churchyard begins with a highly decorative terracotta façade. The row provides a good visual example of contrasting materials and styles of architecture.

Above: St Peter's Churchyard architecture.

Opposite: St Peter's Churchyard: contrasting architecture.

The Grade II-listed County Court and Inland Revenue offices in St Peter's Churchyard, now being used as commercial offices.

Former Boots the Chemist building on the corner of East Street and St Peter's Street.

Almost directly opposite St Peter's Church-yard on the corner of East Street is the former Boots the Chemist shop. This highly decorative Arts and Crafts-style building was designed by Albert Bromley and is adorned with statues commemorating Florence Nightingale, John Lombe, William Hutton and Jedediah Strutt.

Travelling a short distance along East Street will reveal the 1913 Co-operative Society Central Hall, which was designed in a Baroque revival style by Alexander MacPherson.

Florence Nightingale on the façade of the former Boots building.

Co-operative Society Central Hall.

Co-operative Society Central Hall.

The Spot

A rather stylish Art Deco seating area, clock, floral display beds and public convenience, known as The Spot, marks the top of St Peter's Street.

Taxis

To aid visibility of authorised licensed taxis, Derby City Council specified that all Hackney Carriages must be painted AA yellow. This ruling has created a distinctive colour theme on the city's roads.

Taxi rank with the Spot and St Peter's Street in the background.

The Art Deco clock at The Spot.

Westfield Derby

An integral element of Derby's Cityscape regeneration scheme, Westfield Derby is located on the former Castlefields Main Centre. Replacing the old Eagle Centre, Westfield Derby is the largest shopping centre in the East Midlands. This £340 million investment has further enhanced an already vibrant retail sector by encouraging new retail labels and outlets. With approximately 300 retail shops, the centre also boasts a host of customer-friendly facilities, including: adjacent car parking, taxi lounge, bag minding, full disabled access, 12-screen deluxe cinema and a host of local and international restaurants.

Interior views of Westfield.

Interior views of Westfield.

London Road

Leading away from the city centre on the A6 towards the Railway Conservation Area is London Road. This route was formerly the principal road between Carlisle and London. In addition to many of the industrial landmarks, the road is home to the Derbyshire Royal Infirmary, the Liversage Alms Cottages and, further afield, the church of St Osmund's.

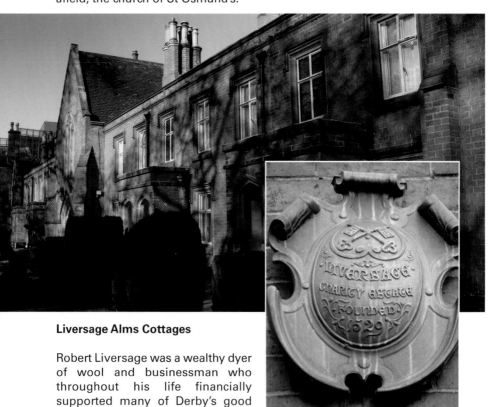

Liversage Alms Cottages

Robert Liversage was a wealthy dyer of wool and businessman who throughout his life financially supported many of Derby's good causes. Having no children, Robert bequeathed the majority of his fortune to benefit the poor of his parish at St Peter's Church. Almshouses were initially constructed in St Peter's Churchyard, but they were later replaced by a further 24 almshouses, a hospital and a chapel on London Road. Designed by the architect John Mason, the project was completed in 1836 and the buildings are now Grade II listed. Under the management of the Liversage Trust, the cottages are still occupied by pensioners who previously lived within the old parish boundaries.

Derbyshire Royal Infirmary

This late 19th-century hospital has associations with Florence Nightingale, who is believed to have provided advice on the design of a replacement building and wards, which were intended to reduce the previously high mortality rates associated with the previous structure. Florence's contribution was recognised when one of the new hospital wings was named after her. Many of the Derbyshire Royal Infirmary (DRI) medical departments have now moved to Derby City General Hospital, leaving the former site to become a community hospital.

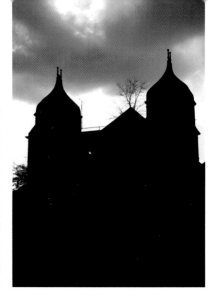

Florence Nightingale Statue

Located on London Road, adjacent to the Derbyshire Royal Infirmary, is a statue commemorating Florence Nightingale. This Grade II-listed monument by sculptress Countess Feodora von Gleichen was unveiled by the Duke of Devonshire in 1914.

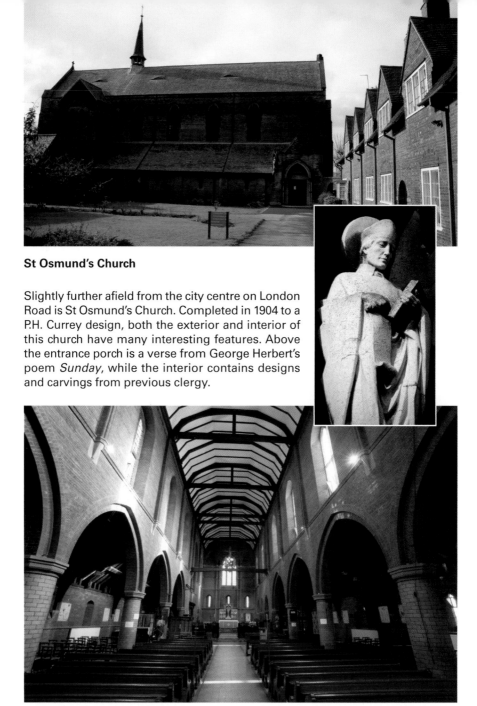

St Osmund's Church

Slightly further afield from the city centre on London Road is St Osmund's Church. Completed in 1904 to a P.H. Currey design, both the exterior and interior of this church have many interesting features. Above the entrance porch is a verse from George Herbert's poem *Sunday*, while the interior contains designs and carvings from previous clergy.

FRIAR GATE CONSERVATION AREA

Designated as Derby's first Conservation Area, Friar Gate, originally known as Markeaton Lane, is said to have inherited its name from a 13th-century Black Friars priory that stood close to the site. Since the Conservation Area was first designated in September 1969, it has been further extended to include other streets nearby. Friar Gate is renowned for its Georgian architecture, and the district is said to contain over 100 listed buildings of historical and architectural interest. In addition to Pickford's House Museum, the area contains other examples of Joseph Pickford's architecture. The religious association is further extended with the nearby Nuns Street and Nun Green, which are said to be named after a former Priory of the Convent of St Mary de Pratis. Friar Gate has many arterial lanes and streets that contain numerous structures and artefacts of historical interest and design merit.

St Werburgh's Church

At the beginning of the western approach to the street from the Wardwick is an 8th-century religious site, on which now stands St Werburgh's Church. The tower of the church is said to date from 1610, while the remainder of the structure was rebuilt to a Sir Arthur Bloomfield design in 1893. Samuel Johnson, famed for his literary works, including the creation of the first English Dictionary, was married at the church in 1735. After many years of being unoccupied, St Werburgh's has now been sensitively converted to a city restaurant.

Opposite: St Werburgh's Church.

Sir Francis Goodwin

Sir Francis Goodwin (1784–1835) is considered one of the most creative designers of early 19th-century churches and was particularly noted for his Gothic revival designs. Friar Gate contains two notable structures by this celebrated architect: the former County Gaol at the top of Vernon Street and the Gothic-style St John's Church on Bridge Street.

Derby County Gaol

A report condemning Derby's ancient prison as being 'insufficient and insecure' prompted the building of Vernon Street Gaol. The Francis Goodwin-designed County Gaol was completed in 1827 at a cost of over £65,000, which was considered a substantial sum for an English gaol at that period. Prompted by the 1931 Reform Act riots, during which the new gaol was besieged by angry mobs, Martello-style towers were added to the façade in 1832. The area in front of the gaol continued to be used for public executions until 1862. After the gaol was demolished in 1928, the land was used as a greyhound track until 1988, when it was sold for the development of offices. All that now remains of the former Derby County Gaol is the imposing Greek Doric façade.

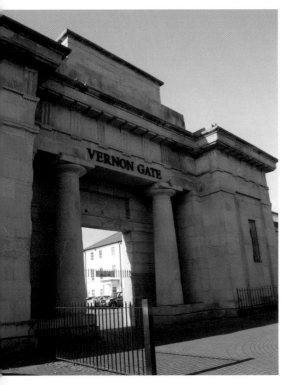

Church of St John the Baptist

The Church of St John the Baptist on Bridge Street was completed in 1828 to a Sir Francis Goodwin design, and is a perfect example of Goodwin's renowned Gothic revival style.

Friar Gate Railway Bridge
Built in 1878, the disused Friar Gate Railway Bridge is a fine example of the renowned local ironsmith Andrew Handyside's work.

Pickfords House Museum

Said to have been constructed by Joseph Pickford for his personal use and as an example of his architectural and building prowess, this 18th-century house is now being utilised as the Pickford's House Museum of Georgian Life and Historic Costume. Further details and images can be found in the museum chapter of this publication.

Derby Gaol Museum

Situated in the cellar of the former 1756 gaol, the museum has restored the Condemned Cell and Debtors Cell. Allegedly haunted, both cells are said to contain the original cell doors, which have graffiti attributed to condemned prisoners. Open to the public at specified times, Derby Gaol is also available to hire for various functions and overnight stays.

Headless Cross

Recorded as being headless since the late 15th-century, the Headless Cross has been relocated to its former market site at Friar Gate. The top of the cross is hollowed and is said to have been filled with vinegar during the 1665 bubonic plague. Money for market transactions would be sterilised in the vinegar.

STRUTT'S PARK CONSERVATION AREA

Designated as one of Derby's Conservation Areas in 1991, Strutt's Park is named after William Strutt, son of the industrialist Jedidiah Strutt. The area contains a significant number of listed and protected structures. Linking St Mary's Church and the Strutt's Park area to the city centre is a footbridge for pedestrians and cyclists, designed by the public art design specialist Dennis O'Connor.

St Mary's Roman Catholic Church

Located just north of Queen Street on Bridge Gate is St Mary's Roman Catholic Church. The foundation stone to this fine Gothic-style church was laid on 4 July 1838, during the same period as Queen Victoria's Coronation, and the building was completed the year after to the design of the renowned architect Augustus W.N. Pugin (1812–1852). An eager exponent of the Gothic revival, he was responsible for the design of many churches, including cathedrals, and various other structures. Pugin has also been credited with the design of Big Ben and the internal decoration of the Palace of Westminster. It has been said that St Mary's is Pugin's finest work and a masterpiece. Indeed, during the Pontifical High Mass Doctor – later Cardinal – Wiseman stated that 'St Mary's, without exception is the most magnificent thing that Catholics have yet done in modern times in this country.'

St Mary's with the St Alkmund footbridge over the inner city ring road in the foreground.

79

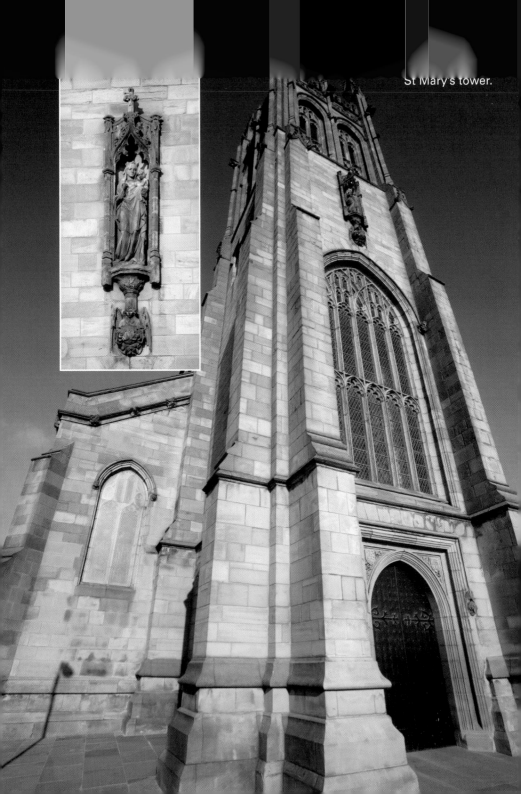

St Mary's tower.

Some of the sculptures and decorations adorning the external walls of St Mary's tower.

St Helen's House

Immediately around the corner from St Mary's and nestled on the fringe of the World Heritage Site is King Street, which contains the Grade I-listed St Helen's House. Designed by local architect Joseph Pickford and completed in 1767, the gentry townhouse originally belonged to the Gisborne family but was eventually purchased by William Strutt. After being converted to a boys' grammar school in 1863 a new extension, known as B Block, and a chapel were eventually added adjacent to the former house. More recently the property has been used as a Community Education Centre.

Portico façade of St Helen's House.

St Helen's House façade masonry.

Grammar school chapel.

Façade of B Block.

Date stone in front of B Block.

Old Derbeians War Memorial

The Old Derbeians War Memorial, in front of St Helen's House, commemorates past school members who lost their lives in conflict.

Overleaf: Old Derbeians War Memorial with St Helen's House behind.

THIS FURTHER INSCRIPTION
COMMEMORATES THOSE
WHO GAVE THEIR LIVES IN
THE SECOND GREAT WAR

1939 – 1945

RAILWAY CONSERVATION AREA

The designation of the Railway Conservation Area in 1979 illustrates the importance that the railway has played in Derby's modern history. Prior to the railway's arrival in the early 19th century, the area was dependent on its road and canal infrastructure to support the transportation of personnel, local produce, raw materials and manufactured goods. One of the original proposals was to site the railway near the Assembly Rooms in the centre of the town. However, it was finally agreed that the three railway companies would share station facilities at the current Railway Terrace site. This was an apparently unusual arrangement and was reportedly the cause of some competitive friction between the three companies: the Midland Counties Railway, the Birmingham and Derby Junction Railway and the North Midlands Railway (NMR). Under intense shareholder pressure, all three companies eventually merged to form the Midland Railway (MR) in 1843.

Although train services began in 1840, the Trijunct Station was not completed until 1841. The station was built to the designs of the renowned North Midland Railway architect Francis Thompson and included an immense platform, which was over 1,000ft long.

Railway Station

Midland Railway Station main entrance.

Midland Hotel

In addition to the station, which was eventually replaced by the Derby Midland Station in 1980, Thompson also designed the surviving Midland Hotel, which was described as 'Accommodation of the Gentry and Nobility'. This high-class hotel was intended for the privileged use of first-class passengers, and many famous people have stayed there, including Queen Victoria, who is reputed to have stayed there several times.

Railway Institute

Created as a cultural centre for railway workers, the Railway Institute was completed in 1892 and contained a library, coffee room, a lecture and concert room and other recreational areas.

Railway Cottages

A triangle of shops, cottages and a public house, designed by Francis Thompson, are believed to be the first-ever railway company purpose-built rail workers' cottages in the country. Despite the inclusion of the Railway Institute in 1894, and a threat to demolish the area for redevelopment, the majority of this Victorian development has been retained and is now protected as a Grade II-listed structure.

Brunswick Inn

Located on the corner of Railway Terrace and Culvert Street, the Brunswick Inn was opened in 1842 for the use of second-class railway passengers and railway workers.

Trijunct Clock

Erected at the end of the railway car park on Railway Terrace is the surviving clock from the entrance of the demolished Trijunct Station.

Midland Road

The conservation area includes the Victorian Midland Road, which is believed to have been constructed to connect London Road with the railway station.

In addition to other historical structures, the road contains the Grade II*-listed Sir Edwin Lutyens-designed Midland Railway War Memorial. Constructed in Portland stone, the memorial was erected in 1922 to commemorate almost 3,000 railway employees who had lost their lives in conflict.

THE CATHEDRAL CHURCH OF ALL SAINTS

Standing at the top of Iron Gate, with its 212ft 16th-century tower, Derby All Saints' Cathedral is one of the city's most prominent landmarks. The former All Saints' Parish Church stands on a site that has provided a place of worship for over 1,000 years.

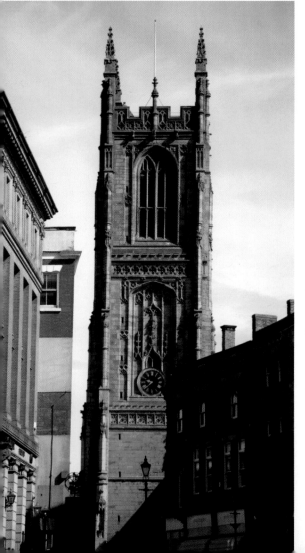

At the turn of the 19th and 20th centuries new dioceses were formed to provide Christian guidance to an ever-increasing population. This event was to be a momentous occasion for All Saints' Church when, on 28 October 1927, it was raised from parish to cathedral status. The predecessor of today's structure was to become practically derelict before a decision to rebuild was made. Built by Francis Smith and designed by James Gibbs (who was also responsible for London's St Mary-le-Strand and St Martin-in-the-Fields), the new church, with its retained early 16th-century adjoining tower, was completed in 1725. Since then there have been further external and internal structural changes, mostly implemented to cope with the increasing local populace and congregation size. The original Robert Bakewell Gate at the tower entrance was sold off during road widening in the late 19th century. However, the current Bakewell gates were from a house demolished nearby on St Mary's Gate.

Bakewell Gate.

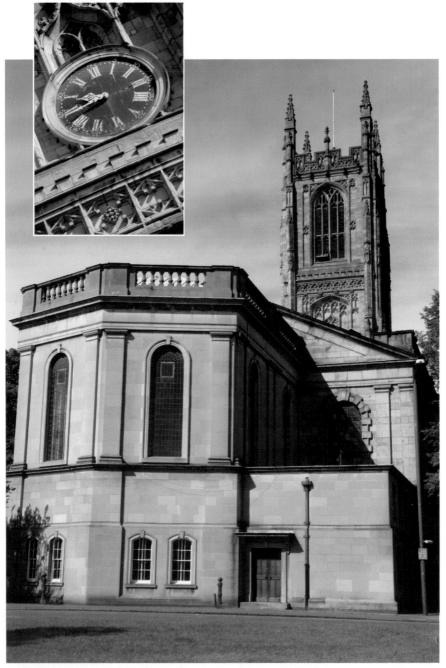

Cathedral Green view of the Sebastian Comper extension.

1972 witnessed the most radical structural change with the completion of an eastern extension, designed by Sebastian Comper. This expansion also allowed some internal redesign, including the repositioning of St Katherine's Chapel to a small and tranquil crypt. A great baldachin (or baldacchinno) over the High Altar and a new Pentelic marble baptismal font were also introduced.

Internal view of the cathedral.

St Katherine's Chapel.

Included in the original internal design was a full-width wrought-iron screen, which was produced by the renowned local iron-smith Robert Bakewell. The screen was initially intended to enrich the appearance of an otherwise simple nave layout, which over a period of time has been subject to repositioning or even removed. Now fully and sympathetically restored, the screen has been repositioned in its original nave location. Decorated with a variety of symbols and crests, the central gates are lavishly adorned with the Royal Arms of George II.

Robert Bakewell Screen.

Opposite: The great baldachin.

Opposite: The cathedral main entrance with the central gallery and Compton organ above.

St Katherine's Quire, on the south side of the cathedral, contains many items of historic and religious interest, including Joseph Wright's tombstone and the Derby Plank. A substantial and lavish monument to Elizabeth, Countess of Shrewsbury, better known as Bess of Hardwick, which she commissioned before her death in 1607, sits above her place of rest.

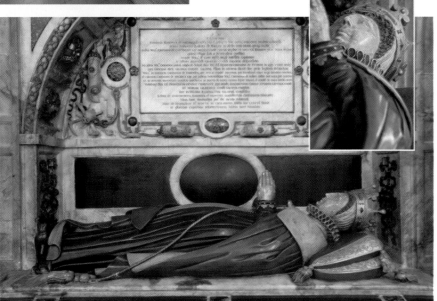

Bess of Hardwick Monument.

The Derby Plank.

The two coloured-glass windows by the Welsh artist Ceri Richards.

RIVER DERWENT

The city of Derby undoubtedly owes its settlement origins and industrial prosperity to the River Derwent. Spectacular scenery surrounds the 80km-long waterway, which is Derbyshire's longest river. Its picturesque route from its source to the River Trent passes through the grounds of Chatsworth Estate and encounters the reservoirs of Howden, Derwent and Ladybower.

The river's force was harnessed to power the Derwent Valley Mills, which are now a World Heritage Site. Its passage through Derby is lined with views of ancient churches, a cathedral, cotton and silk mills, city parks and gardens, public art and wildlife habitats. Now being appreciated for its aesthetic rather than industrial value, the river and its banks offer residents and visitors abundant leisure and sporting opportunities, including walking, cycling, fishing and rowing.

Boar's Head Cotton Mill

Constructed by the Evans family in the late 18th and early 19th century, Boar's Head Cotton Mill represents one of the most complete mill complexes within the Derwent Valley World Heritage Site. The mill buildings are still in use for a variety of commercial purposes.

Boar's Head Cotton Mill

Darley Playing Fields

A popular walking, cycling and sporting venue, Darley Playing Fields runs parallel with the river and is just one of over 300 public open spaces within the city.

Rowing

The riverside is home to both the Derwent and Derby rowing clubs.

Handyside Bridge

Part of the original Great Northern Railway line, the Grade II-listed Handyside Bridge was constructed in 1877 by the renowned foundry Andrew Handyside & Co.

The Chapel of St Mary on the Bridge

Located on the banks of the River Derwent, the Chapel of St Mary on the Bridge is one of only six remaining bridge chapels in England. Although the site has housed a chapel for many centuries, the current structure primarily dates from the 15th century. Other than its original and current religious origins, the chapel has been utilised for many other purposes, including private dwellings, hosiery works, and carpenters' workshops. Replacing an earlier priest's residence, the adjoining Bridge Chapel House was added during the 17th century. The original connecting mediaeval bridge was demolished, with its successor being constructed slightly upstream, severing the chapel from its ancient origins.

Serious deterioration in the late 1920s threatened the chapel's survival. Timely intervention by the Haslam family provided funds for the purchase of the site and a sensitive restoration project was undertaken as a memorial to their father, Sir Alfred Seal Haslam, a former Mayor of Derby. Further repair work throughout the 20th century has ensured that this enchanting and intimate place of worship continues to serve its original purpose, albeit without its bridge.

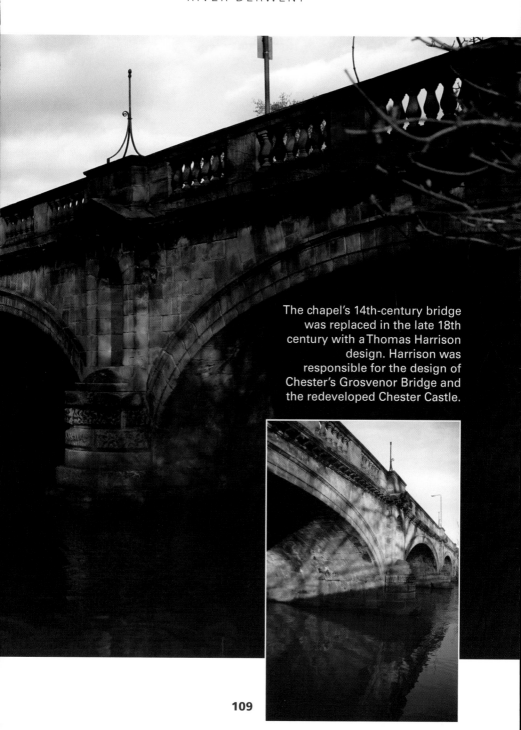

The chapel's 14th-century bridge was replaced in the late 18th century with a Thomas Harrison design. Harrison was responsible for the design of Chester's Grosvenor Bridge and the redeveloped Chester Castle.

Exeter Bridge

Situated over the River Derwent on Derwent Street, Exeter Bridge was opened in 1931 as part of the Central Improvement Plan, which also included the relocation of the market and the eventual construction of a new town hall. The bridge was initially designed by Charles Arthur Clews, but was completed by the Borough Architect Charles Aslin. Each corner of the bridge contains a bas-relief of prominent Derbeians: Erasmus Darwin, Herbert Spencer, William Hutton and John Lombe.

Bas-relief of William Hutton on Exeter Bridge.

Riverside Gardens

A favoured haunt of city workers during lunch breaks, the Riverside Gardens offers respite from the bustling city centre. Facing onto the river, this attractive public space lies between Exeter Bridge and the St Alkmund's flyover.

Boy and the Ram

Part of the Derby public artwork scheme, the Boy and the Ram statue, by the artist Wilfred Dudeney, is located in the Riverside Gardens.

Weir with the cathedral in the background.

DERBY MUSEUMS

Derby's natural history, creative heritage, industrial inheritance and architectural grandeur is aesthetically presented and preserved for present and future generations, at each of the three Derby City Council-managed museums.

Derby Museum and Art Gallery

Derby Museum and Art Gallery can be accessed via various routes on the Strand and Wardwick. However, the Wardwick entrance offers a fitting passage to the gallery's impressive upper-floor collections. Completed in 1879 to an R.K. Freeman design, the Gothic-style frontage, with a tall Franco-Flemish tower, was gifted to the city by the brewer and philanthropist Michael Thomas Bass.

Although this route is the principal access to the city's Central Library, the entrance stairway also leads to the museum's first floor. The staircase contains various sculptures and busts, all of which are colourfully backlit by a bowed, street-fronted, stained-glass window.

Bonnie Prince Charlie

The contribution of Charles Edward Stuart, better known as Bonnie Prince Charlie, to Derby's heritage is appropriately represented in a dramatically lit and appropriately furnished room. A recorded narration relates how, in December 1745, the Young Pretender decided to abandon his quest to become king of England, beating a retreat from Derby back to Scotland and facing his final defeat at Culloden.

If the prince had ignored false intelligence and convinced his troops to advance on London, then the political and ecclesiastical history of the England, Europe and perhaps the world would have been dramatically altered on that night in Derby. The authenticity of the exhibition room is further enhanced by the inclusion of the oak panels from Exeter House, where the Prince resided while in Derby. The panels were yet another gift from the museum's benefactor, Michael Thomas Bass.

Bonnie Prince Charlie statue

A life-size statue of the prince on horseback, by the sculpture Anthony Stones, was unveiled in 1995 and proudly stands at the rear of the cathedral on Cathedral Green.

Museum collections

The museum has an extensive range of interesting exhibitions relating to archaeology, history, local military regiments, geology and wildlife. However, the History of Derby Porcelain and the Joseph Wright of Derby collections are particularly worthy of special mention.

Secrets of the Mummies exhibition.

118

Derbyshire Nature exhibition.

The Repton Stone

Part of the Origins of Derby collection, this 8th-century Anglo-Saxon cross once stood outside the church at Repton.

Joseph Wright of Derby

Joseph Wright (1734–1797) studied art in London before eventually returning to his native Derby to become an established landscape and portrait painter. As some of his works portray, the artist was fascinated by the sciences and befriended many local industrialists and academics, including Josiah Wedgwood and Erasmus Darwin. Indeed, he is believed to be one of the principal artists capturing and conveying scenes relating to both science and industry during the period of the Industrial Revolution. Although Wright's works have an international appeal and are exhibited globally, Derby Art Gallery is said to possess and display the largest collection of the artist's paintings, including the renowned *A Philosopher Lecturing on the Orrery.*

Opposite: Close-up view of an Orrery.

Orrery

An orrery is a mechanical device, in this case clockwork, used to illustrate the motion of the planets in relation to their solar system.

The Joseph Wright exhibition room
with an orrery in the foreground.

Derby Porcelain exhibition.

3 Coffee cup
and saucer.
Derby porcelain
Pattern no.66.
About 1785-1790

Pickford's House Museum

Constructed during the late 18th century, Pickford's House Museum of Georgian Life and Historic Costume is located on Derby's Friar Gate. As the architect, builder and first owner, Joseph Pickford is said to have designed the house as an illustration of his architectural and building prowess. Indeed, Pickford was responsible for many architectural projects throughout Derby and the Midlands, including a prized commission to build a factory near Stoke-on-Trent for the celebrated potter Josiah Wedgwood.

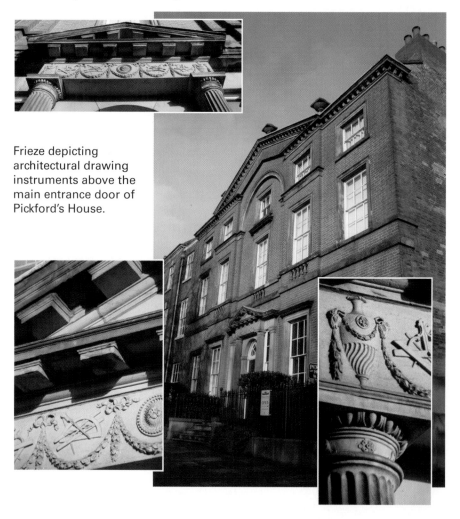

Frieze depicting architectural drawing instruments above the main entrance door of Pickford's House.

Cellar, kitchen and scullery.

Exploration of the museum's different display floors offers an upstairs and downstairs perspective of life as a scullery maid, servant or master. The following images illustrate a selection of the many intriguing displays and rooms within the museum.

The largest cellar on the kitchen and scullery floor was converted to a World War Two air-raid shelter by the Schofield family. The cellar contains many of the accoutrements deemed essential for survival, or basic comfort, during a potential bombing raid.

Air-raid shelter.

An impressive ground floor entrance hall leads to elegantly furnished dining, drawing and morning rooms which represent how the house may have looked during the Pickford family's residence.

Entrance hallway.

Morning room.

Dining room.   Master Bedroom.

The first floor contains further displays and furnished rooms, including an Edwardian bathroom with elaborate shower and decorative porcelain. A dedicated children's playroom allows young visitors to amuse themselves with a variety of playful distractions, including a large dolls' house complete with scaled furniture.

Children's playroom.   Edwardian bathroom.

Opposite: Drawing room.

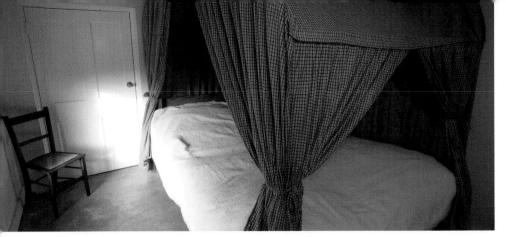

Servant's bedroom.

The top floor aptly illustrates the bare living essentials normally associated with a servant's bedroom. An adjoining room houses an unusual collection of elaborately and colourfully clad dressed toy theatres.

In addition to its permanent collections, there are also a variety of temporary exhibitions which are normally pertinent to the general theme and period of the museum. At the time of publication, entry to all exhibits is free, but the museum should be contacted to confirm opening times and current exhibitions.

Toy theatre collection.

Derby's Museum of Industry and History –
The Silk Mill

Derby's Museum of Industry and History, also referred to as the Silk Mill, is located on the site of what is considered to be the world's first modern factory – a title attributed to the fact that all the factory manufacturing processes were executed from a single source of power, the water wheel.

Silk Mill

Constructed by George Sorocold for the Lombe brothers in the early 18th century, the mill originally contained machinery for the manufacture of silk thread produced by a silk-throwing process. The site was deliberately located on the banks of the River Derwent to enable the silk-twisting machinery to be powered by a mill wheel. Prior to the construction of this factory the manufacture of silk thread was dominated by the Italians. While working in Italy in the silk thread industry, in a daring act of industrial espionage, John Lombe made drawings of the complex Italian silk-spinning machinery. It was an act which eventually cost him his life in 1722 when he died of a mysterious illness, thought to be caused by poison administered by a female Italian assassin working on behalf of the Italian silk thread manufacturers. However, despite arrest the suspected assassin was released due to lack of evidence.

Throughout its history, the Silk Mill has been subjected to alteration, demolition and fire. Integral to the Derwent Valley Hills World Heritage Site, sections of the original factory bell tower and foundations are still visible.

Attached to the mill is a set of gates produced in 1725 by the local ironsmith Robert Bakewell.

Rebuilt after a 1910 fire, the building was used for the manufacturing of chemist products before becoming an electric meter repair facility. Derby's Museum of Industry and History opened its doors at the Silk Mill in 1974. Exhibitions of local life and industry include a World Heritage Site Room, Railway Engineering and Research, Power for Industry, Derbyshire Industries, Rolls-Royce and temporary displays.

Robert Bakewell gates.

Surviving bell tower.

Animated model of John Lombe with voice narration.

Framework Knitter's Cottage exhibition.

Narrow fabrics loom.

The Midland Railway Study Centre and Railway Engineering Exhibition.

The George Fletcher Grasshopper Steam Engine within the Power for Industry exhibition.

The Rolls Royce RB211
aero engine.

Rolls-Royce exhibition.

Another photograph of the RB211 aero engine.

Rolls-Royce Griffon aero engine.

CREATIVE INDUSTRIES

With a host of renowned porcelain artists, painters, ironsmiths and architects, Derby already possesses a rich creative heritage. The creative sector encompasses a vast range of disciplines, ranging from the traditional skills associated with art and fabric design, through to the more modern fields of digital imaging and software graphics. Dedicated business units at Friar Gate Studios and Derby University's Banks' Mill are just two examples of how Derby intends to support and promote the growth of this vital sector of employment. The Quad in the Market Place adds further fertility to the city's ambition to become the creative capital of the midlands.

Banks' Mill

Described as a University of Derby business incubation unit, Banks' Mill Studios are located in the West End's Bridge Street. This converted rope works building was established to support the development of new businesses in the creative sector. The facility offers budding artistic entrepreneurs studio space and support services. With approximately 38 studios and artists, the mill hosts periodical 'Open Studio' events, where visitors are invited to browse or buy a vast range of unique artwork, jewellery, glassware, photography, ceramics, textiles, sculptures, poetry and much more.

Laura Ellen Bacon, a visual artist of contemporary forms in willow is a former Banks' Mills Studio resident artist.

Banks' Mill resident artist Sara Taylor is a ceramics artist and also a designer of English Fine Bone China.

Examples of the jewellery and fabrics designed by Banks' Mill artists.

Friar Gate Studios

Friar Gate Studios has space for approximately 40 businesses. This modern purpose-built facility offers fledgling creative businesses working studio space and a host of supporting amenities. A City Council initiative which clearly demonstrates the importance that Derby places on the creative industries.

140

DERBY MARKETS

In 1154 King Henry II granted Derby a Royal Charter to run weekly markets and periodical fairs. Derby was granted a second Royal Charter by King John in 1204. The granting of a Royal Charter was considered an honour and undoubtedly aided the prosperity and growth of the settlement. The city has retained its commercial inheritance and roots with a thriving market-based community.

Guildhall entrance to the Market Hall.

Two large city-centre indoor markets – with another slightly further afield at Allenton – are complimented by periodical local farmers' and continental markets in the Market Place. Frequent commercial farming livestock and wholesale markets lend support to Derby's flourishing market economy. The ancient tradition of the council officially appointing an annual 'Pinder and Tenter' still prevails, with the Pinder being responsible for rounding up any stray market animals and securing them in the pinfold. The Tenter was traditionally a clothmaker who erected the cloth pens that held the animals in place on market days. The appointment is normally awarded unopposed to the incumbent Market Manager.

Market Hall

Situated in the Cathedral Quarter of the city, Derby Market Hall was completed in 1866 as a replacement for its predecessor. The indoor Victorian market was designed by the Borough Surveyor T.C. Thorburn, but it was completed, with some design modifications, by George Thompson. An impressive iron-vaulted roof, by the engineer Rowland Ordish, covers a balcony and ground-floor array of stalls, with dedicated fish and poultry areas. Many of the stallholders have traded their wares for decades and some are second-generation family businesses, all of which add to the convenience and friendly ambience of the Market Hall.

The Osnabrück Square entrance to the Market Hall.

Osnabrück Square entrance

Named after Derby's twin town of Osnabrück, the civic square offers access to the Market Hall.

Derby signed a partnership treaty with the German city of Osnabrück in 1976. The cities are said to be twinned because of their relative geographical and industrial similarities, and also their differences.

Osnabrück Square commemoration milestone.

Ted Corden of R. & L. Fruits Greengrocers, one of the stallholders at Derby Market Hall.

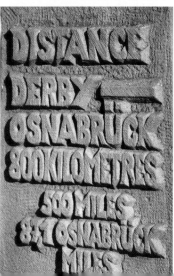

143

Opposite: Flowers and fish produce adjacent to the entrance of the Market Hall.

Eagle Market

Named from the crest of a previous landowner, this 1970s redevelopment scheme required the demolition of early 19th-century residential properties. Developed to replace an open-air market at Morledge, the area originally encompassed a shopping precinct, new

playhouse and market. The market also offers direct access to Westfield.

Fresh fruit and vegetables, confectionery, cheese and fabrics are just a few of the numerous products and services being offered in the bustling Eagle Market.

Eagle Market produce.

Cattle Market

Relocated to a purpose-built site on Chequers Road in 1970, Derby continues its ancient tradition of livestock markets, including a twice-monthly horse market with associated farming stalls and products.

DERBY ECONOMY

Easy access to an abundance of local raw materials, geographical position and entrepreneurial leadership all contributed to Derby's worldwide reputation as a major instigator of the Industrial Revolution.

The city continues to prosper as a successful hi-technology-based manufacturing region within many of its traditional and new industries, including aerospace, railway engineering, car production, clockmaking and high-quality porcelain industries. Derby's industrial diversity is a tribute to the flexibility and ingenuity of its workforce and entrepreneurs.

This chapter concentrates on just three of Derby's many manufacturing industries, illustrating how quality and craftsmanship will ensure survival in a highly competitive global marketplace.

Rolls-Royce

Founded by Fredrick Henry Royce and Charles Stewart Rolls in 1906, Rolls-Royce is arguably one of the most eminent engineering names in the world. The history of this prestigious company and its founders is well documented. Famed for both its car and aero engine production, the company's long association with Derby has further enhanced the city's engineering and economic profile.

Rolls-Royce Moor Lane site.

A purpose-built factory sited at Osmaston was completed to Henry Royce's own design in 1907, with production starting in July of the following year. Diversification into aero engine production was facilitated both by Charles Rolls's passion for aviation, and by a demand to supply World War One aero engines to the Ministry of Defence. Rolls died tragically in an aviation accident in 1910. Throughout the first half of the 20th century the company continued to expand and open new manufacturing facilities to accommodate both car and aero engine production. However, it was the demand for the Rolls-Royce Merlin engine during the World War Two that transformed the relatively small company into a major competitor in the aero engine industry. In addition to powering the World War Two Hurricane and Spitfire aircraft, Merlin engines were also used in the Lancaster Bomber and (built under licence by Packard) the American P-51 Mustang. Many believe that without the ingenuity and productivity of Derby's Rolls-Royce workforce the Battle of Britain, and the eventual outcome of the war, may well have taken a different course.

Rolls-Royce's success during World War Two ensured that both Derby and the aero engine production facilities were a primary target for the German Luftwaffe. Many electronic and physical measures were taken to thwart the bombing raids, including painting and camouflaging factory facilities. Ernest Townsend (1880–1944), an eminent Derby portrait and landscape painter, was employed to ensure that the Rolls-Royce factory was painted to resemble a village when viewed from the air.

Moving car manufacturing to Crewe in 1946 ensured that the Derby facility was dedicated to aero engine production.

The latter half of the 20th century brought a fascinating rollercoaster tale of near bankruptcy, nationalisation, privatisation, global expansion and diversification into other engineering disciplines and markets making Rolls-Royce the global leader it is today.

Sir Henry Royce Statue

Sculpted by Derwent Wood in 1921, the statue of Sir Henry Royce has previously been sited at the Arboretum and Riverside Gardens. Now located at Rolls-Royce's Moor Lane facility, the statue bears a plaque giving details of Royce's life.

Sir Henry Royce statue at Moor Lane.

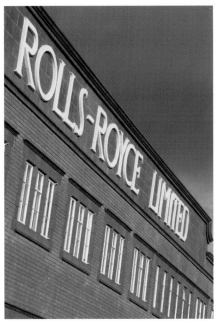

Nightingale Road

Nightingale Road was the site of Derby's first Rolls-Royce factory and was completed to a design by Henry Royce, with the central section of the façade being added in 1938. After over 100 years of production the Nightingale Road site is no longer being used by Rolls-Royce.

Aero engine production line at Wilmore Road.

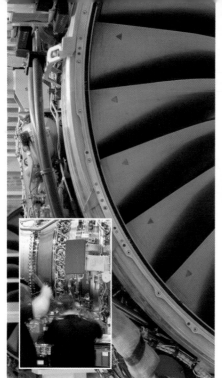

Aero engine test facility at Wilmore Road.

Aero repair and overhaul facility at Sinfin.

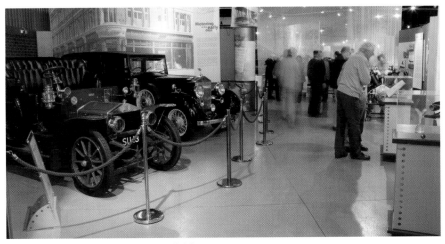

Rolls-Royce Heritage Trust exhibition entrance.

Rolls-Royce Heritage Trust

The Rolls-Royce Heritage Trust exhibition is housed within the Learning and Development Centre on Wilmore Road. The exhibition displays an impressive collection of artefacts relating to the company's manufacturing history. Although not open for general public access, it is possible to view the exhibition by prior appointment.

A 10hp two-cylinder 1907 Rolls-Royce with a 25/30hp 1936 Rolls-Royce in the background.

The Spirit of Ecstasy on the radiator grille of a 25/30hp 1936 Rolls-Royce.

A 10hp two-cylinder 1907 Rolls-Royce.   *Opposite:* The Spirit of Ecstasy.

The Eagle

The company's first aero engine, the Eagle, was manufactured in 1914 and was used to power the first transatlantic flight.

The Eagle aero engine.

Various Heritage Trust exhibits.

Royal Crown Derby

Although Royal Crown Derby has been manufacturing porcelain at its Osmaston Road factory since 1877, the company's production legacy dates from approximately 1750.

The foundation of the porcelain company is attributed to a partnership between a potter, a painter and a banker. André Planché, a maker of soft-paste porcelain vases, together with porcelain painter William Duesbury, teamed up with banker John Heath to form Derby Porcelain. William Duesbury eventually assumed sole control and ownership of the company, and under his shrewd entrepreneurial guidance the company prospered.

Over 250 years of porcelain production offers a fascinating story of evolving products, diversification, designs and styles. Equally enthralling are the personal histories of the factory's various owners, which occasionally contrast greatly with the inspirational leadership of its founder William Duesbury.

The incorporation of a crown into the Derby porcelain name is attributed to King George III, who in 1775 instructed Duesbury to include the royal crown insignia in the company's name and hence its trademark. Crown Derby Porcelain was again honoured when, in 1890, Queen Victoria issued a Royal Warrant appointing the company 'Manufacturers of Porcelain to Her Majesty', allowing it to change its name to 'Royal Crown Derby Porcelain'. The foundation and success of the Osmaston factory site expanded to include a former workhouse building, which although modernised continues to play host to many of the porcelain manufacturing processes.

A major employer within the city, Royal Crown Derby continues to prosper and flourish. The company presently creates a range of exceptionally high quality prestige bone china giftware, tableware and collectables, all of which are highly desirable with a global customer appeal.

Factory Shop
The factory shop within the Royal Crown Derby porcelain production factory at Osmaston Road.

Crown on top of the main factory and visitors' centre façade at Osmaston Road.

Guided Tour

Royal Crown Derby offers a highly recommended guided tour of the Osmaston Road factory. Visitors will observe meticulous attention to detail, with each stage of the production process adding further craftsmanship, quality and value. The visit is further enhanced by demonstration displays, a museum, restaurant and well-stocked factory shop.

Royal Crown Derby porcelain production process at Osmaston Road.

Royal Crown Derby porcelain production process at Osmaston Road.

Porcelain Artists

Royal Crown Derby employs highly talented artists to create unique porcelain pieces, which are commissioned to the customer's specific requirements.

Royal Crown Derby factory shop.

250ᵗʰ Anniversary Fountain

The year 2000 was the 250th anniversary of Royal Crown Derby's first recorded production of a porcelain piece. Designed by John Ablitt, Royal Crown Derby's 250th anniversary fountain is located in the main entrance to the factory and visitors' centre on Osmaston Road. This is the largest piece ever produced by the prestige porcelain designers, which contains the familiar Royal Crown Derby cobalt blue colour and 24 carat burnished gold.

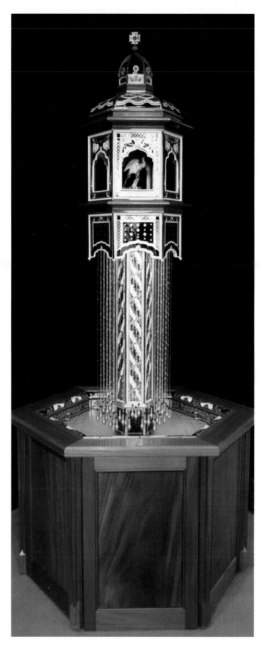

Smith of Derby

As an apprentice to the renowned Whitehurst family of clockmakers, John Smith began trading as an independent clockmaker in 1856. With over 160 years of experience in the clock manufacturing industry, the company has established itself as the oldest family-owned clockmakers in Britain and number one in the world. With its undisputed reputation for craftsmanship, quality and innovative design, Smith of Derby has a global customer base for both its traditional and contemporary timepieces. Located in Alfreton Road, Smith's are also responsible for the renovation and restoration of many historic and modern landmark clocks.

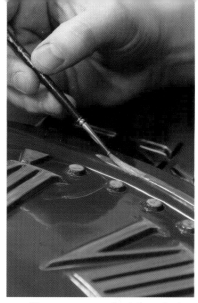

New concave clock face being prepared for gold leaf.

Winding mechanisms ready for testing.

Completed clock ready for dispatch.

Traditional and modern clock faces.

Clock restoration.

MAYOR OF DERBY

Under a charter granted by Charles I in 1637, Derby became responsible for its own governance and replaced its elected bailiffs with a Mayor. Elected annually, the Mayor's legal and civic responsibilities for the borough have diminished over the centuries to that of a primarily representative and ceremonial role.

Mayor of Derby 2007–08, Councillor Pauline Latham, OBE.

The Mayor of Derby's Attendant Serjeant at Mace, Alan Taylor, carrying the 1637 ceremonial mace.

The Mayor of Derby's chain of office.

Ceremonial mace.

Ceremonial sword.

Completed in the 1940s under the Charles Aslin Central Improvements Scheme, the Council House's impressive portico entrance on Corporation Street leads, via a ceremonial staircase, to the Council Chambers, Civic Suite and Mayor's Parlour.

Memorabilia of Derby's past glories and heritage lines the route, including lavishly decorated Royal Crown Derby Freeman of the Borough caskets and, signifying Derby's long association with the Senior Service, a Royal Navy ship's wheel from HMS *Kenya*, a cruiser adopted by Derby in 1942.

Ceremonial staircase with HMS *Kenya* ship's wheel.

Royal Crown Derby Freeman of the Borough caskets were awarded to individuals for eminent and distinguished service.

Mayor's Parlour

Lined with oak panelling, rescued from Derwent Hall before the villages of Derwent and Ashopton were submerged to form the Ladybower Reservoir, the Mayor's Parlour contains a plethora of ceremonial regalia. Almost every item in this civic office has historic significance and an associated story to tell.

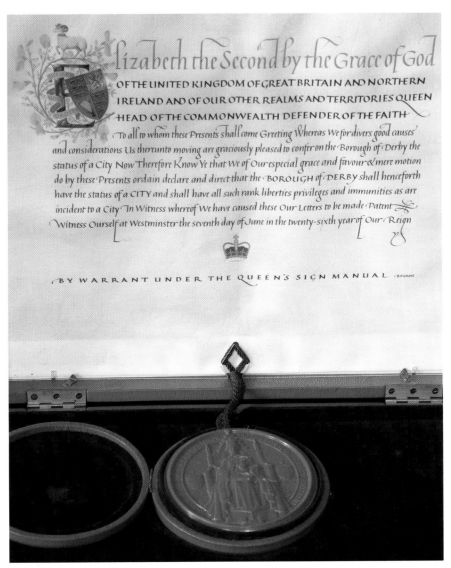

Royal Charter of 1977

Delivered by HM Queen Elizabeth II to the Mayor of Derby during a visit in July 1977, the Royal Sign Manual, granting Derby city status on 7 June 1977, resides in the Mayor's Parlour.

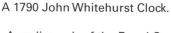

A 1790 John Whitehurst Clock.

A replica pair of the Royal Crown Derby bowls presented to Derby's twinned city of Osnabrück to celebrate the German city's 1200th anniversary.

Civic Suite

Used for the entertaining of guests and dignitaries, the Art Deco-style suite is also licensed to perform civil marriages and partnerships.

UNIVERSITY OF DERBY

The formation of the Derbyshire College of Further Education resulted from the merger of Derby Lonsdale College of Higher Education and the Derby Municipal Technical College. Each of these institutions could trace its origins to the 1850s and they were both the result of progressive amalgamations. From its formation in 1983 the Derbyshire College of Further Education strived to gain polytechnic status and was finally rewarded in 1992 when it was designated as the University of Derby. Divided among four faculties, the university offers an impressive portfolio of further education, undergraduate and postgraduate courses, with academic subjects ranging from art, technology, sciences and health, to business and law. Delivering education and training from a number of new and restored campuses within the city, the university also has additional facilities at Buxton. Derby University's main campus is situated on Kedleston Road in the vicinity of Markeaton Park – other buildings make up what is now called the University Quarter.

Library and Learning Centre.

Atrium architecture and teaching facilities.

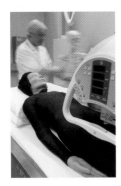

The GE Healthcare Imaging Suite at the Education, Health and Sciences Faculty.

In addition to the educational facilities, the campus caters for students' cultural, religious and social needs.

Multi-faith Centre at the Kedleston Road Campus.

Student bar and recreation area.

Opened in 2007, the University of Derby's Markeaton Street Campus is home to a purpose-built £21 million arts, design, media and technology teaching facility.

Markeaton Street
Campus.

Textile design training facilities.

Students on a fashion design course.

Digital Video and Digital Photography Media Suite.

Graduation ceremony in the Assembly Rooms Great Hall.

DERBY COUNTY FOOTBALL CLUB

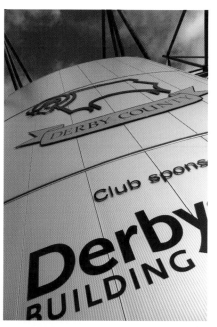

Formed in 1884, and one of the founding members of the Football League, Derby County Football Club moved from their historic Baseball Ground to a purpose-built stadium at Pride Park in 1997. Nicknamed the Rams, the club has a proud record of memorable football achievements, including winning the Football Association Cup (FA Cup) in 1946 and the Football Association League Championship in 1972 and again in 1975. Additionally, the club has made many appearances in European Football competitions and reached the semi-finals of the European Cup in 1973.

HAUNTED DERBY

Nicknamed the 'Ghost Capital of Britain', Derby's ghoulish reputation is supported by numerous personal accounts of spectre sightings. Derby Gaol, situated in Friar Gate, offers a series of ghost walk tours and overnight vigils.

Derby Gaol.

Ghost tour at the Old Bell Hotel in Saddler Gate.

Ghost tour at the Fish Market near Cornmarket.

DERBY PARKS AND RECREATION

Ranging from the inner-city Waterside Gardens to the large open spaces of Markeaton Park, Derby boasts over 300 areas of public open spaces. Covering over 2,000 acres of land, members of the public have open access to an abundance of inner-city suburban and rural recreational, leisure and sporting facilities.

Allestree Park

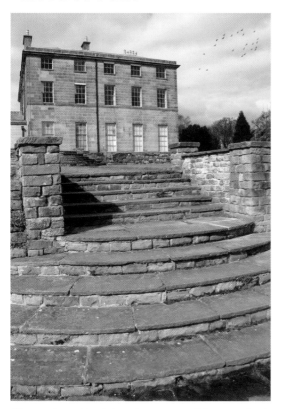

Situated north of the city centre, Allestree Park contains a fishing lake, 18-hole golf course and the Grade II-listed Allestree Hall. Catering for a family day out, the park boasts a number of walks plus a pets corner and fish pond.

Darley Abbey Park

Stretching north from the edge of the city centre and running adjacent to the River Derwent for approximately one mile is Darley Abbey Park. Officially opened by HRH Prince George in 1931, the park was landscaped by William Evans and donated to the public by the Evans family. With the exception of the Darley Abbey Inn, there are only a few remaining traces of the park's founding 12th-century monastic forefathers. The park contains many interesting features, which include a walled garden, the National Collection of Viburnum and Hydrangea, Butterfly Garden, Darley Tree Trail, café and children's play area.

Markeaton Park

At over 200 acres in size, Markeaton is one of Derby's largest parks. Located less than two miles north-west of the city centre, the former deer park was the 16th-century home of the Mundy family. Partially donated and council-purchased, the grounds were officially opened by HRH Prince George in 1931, with an enlarged fishing and boating lake being opened a few years later by Edward, Prince of Wales.

Although the 1755 Markeaton Hall was demolished in 1964, the Joseph Pickford-designed Orangery and stable yard, which were added to the hall in the late 18th century, still survive as a café and craft village.

The park grounds are home to a very impressive array of facilities and events including a light railway, fishing, boating, café, floral displays, football and cricket pitches, tennis courts plus a dedicated purpose-built area for roller and skateboard enthusiasts.

The popular Mundy Play Centre provides an imaginative array of children's playground equipment.

The Orangery.

Markeaton Craft Village.

Stream.

Lake and park grounds.

Lake with swans and ducks.

Derby Arboretum

The occasion of the opening of England's first specifically designed public park on Wednesday 16 September 1840 is well documented. At an official presentation in the Town Hall Joseph Strutt, a mill owner and former Mayor of Derby (1835), gifted the Arboretum to the people of Derby. On completion of the ceremony the whole town is said to have taken the afternoon off work and formed a long processional parade, headed by Joseph Strutt, to the park for a grand opening ceremony. Philanthropist Strutt wanted to offer the people of Derby a place for education, recreation and exercise. However, despite Strutt's benevolence, the cost of maintaining the park meant that free entry was only available to all on Wednesday and Sunday, and a charge was levied on all other days. The entry fee was eventually abolished in 1882.

Designed by John Claudius Loudon, it is believed that the Arboretum was the inspiration for the design of New York's Central Park. To create a feeling of space on the 11-acre site, mounds of earth were deliberately used to hide the views of other paths and the park boundaries. As a place where trees, shrubs and herbaceous plants are cultivated for educational and scientific purposes, Strutt instructed that no same two species of tree should be planted, which would encourage visitors to walk around the whole park.

During World War Two a bomb blast destroyed a bandstand and earthenware statue known as the Florentine Boar, which had originally resided in Strutt's garden. The City Council commissioned A.W. Paxton to sculpt a bronze replica of the Florentine Boar and in November 2005 the sculpture was reinstated in the park.

Entrance lodge viewed from
the park.

Left: Entrance lodge at
Arboretum Street.

Far Left: Florentine Boar.

A tradition of patting or rubbing the boar's nose swiftly became customary among the local population and informed visitors.

An additional entrance lodge at Arboretum Street, designed by Henry Duesbury, was erected by the town council in 1850. The lodge includes a memorial statue of Joseph Strutt handing over the deeds of the park to the town council.

In recognition of its importance the Derby Arboretum, and its extended area, has been designated as Grade II*-listed and is a Derby Conservation Area.

Little Chester

Believed to be the site of the Roman settlement Derventio, Chester Green is part of the Little Chester Conservation Area. The site is used for sport recreation and has two football fields.

Every spring there is a mass of daffodils along the edge of Chester Green.

ACKNOWLEDGEMENTS

We would like to acknowledge the contribution and support of the following individuals and organisations that have so very kindly provided assistance during the writing of this book. Without their extensive co-operation we would not have been able to create such a varied portfolio of images of the city of Derby.

Gary Atkins, Andrew Auld, Anneke Banberry, Stella Birks, Simon Butt, Dawn Dagley, Derby Markets' staff and stallholders, Derby Museum staff, Andy Falconer, Ed Felix, Collette Flood, Paul Joels, Mayor of Derby – Councillor Pauline Latham, OBE, Derek Limer, Caroline Lucy, Reverend Canon Donald Macdonald, Linda McFarland, Faye Nixon, Phil O'Brien, Simon Pank, Filomena Rodriguez and Banks' Mill Studio residents, Alex Smith, Adam Tamsett, Alan Taylor and Dennis Wardle.

Assembly Rooms
Banks' Mill Studios
BBC Radio Derby
Cattle Market
Derby Cathedral
Derby City Council
Derby County Football Club
Derby Ghost Walks
Derby Market Hall
Derby Museum and Art Gallery
Eagle Market
Marketing Derby
Mayor of Derby
Pickford's House Museum
Rolls-Royce plc
Royal Crown Derby
Smith of Derby Ltd
St Osmund's Church
The Guildhall
The Silk Mill
University of Derby
Westfield Derby